Rustington
in old picture postcards

Mary Taylor

Best Wishes
Mary Taylor

European Library   ZALTBOMMEL / THE NETHERLANDS

GB ISBN 90 288 6653 1

© 2001 European Library – Zaltbommel/The Netherlands

European Library
post office box 49
NL – 5300 AA Zaltbommel/The Netherlands
telephone: 0031 418 513144
fax: 0031 418 515515
e-mail:publisher@eurobib.nl

Introduction

Rustington lies between the South Downs to the north and the English Channel to the south, it is situated in West Sussex, 5 miles south-west of Arundel and 7 miles west of Worthing, and the whole area is flat and ideal for walking.

The name Rustington allegedly derives from the time of the Saxon occupation of the area. Finds found in the archaeological excavations in Rustington in 1986/1987 have proved that it has had continuous occupation from the Mesolithic period, through the Bronze Age, Iron Age, Roman and Mediaeval periods, right up to the present day, with artefacts and coins still being unearthed.

The earliest building extant in Rustington is the Parish Church of St. Peter and St. Paul, it is of the 11th century and is said to be on the site of an earlier church.

Until the middle of the 19th century, life appears to have changed little, governed as it was by the feudal system of the manorial lords. Things were to change, however, with the coming of the railway and Angmering Station in 1846. Brickyards opened up to serve the growing building industry and later, nurseries took over a lot of the large farms, which were split into smaller units for the growing of greenhouse crops etc.

The first little church school was opened in 1859 to cater for sixty children, we now have three large primary schools in Rustington. Mr. John Simpson, a baker, opened the first village shop in Sea Lane between 1833 and 1840. The village really 'woke up' during the First World War, with the arrival of hundreds of Canadian and American servicemen, when they began the construction of the American Air Station, this was on what is now known as the Sea Estate. This airstation was for the training centre, for the 0/400 Handley Page bomber, but did not become fully operational due to the ending of the war.

So the village grew, from a population of 616 in 1901, 3,897 in 1951, 8,904 in 1971 to 13,000 in 2001. The 1960s saw the start of the population explosion and the intense building development throughout the village.

Still to be found in the Old World part of the village are, 17th- and 18th-century houses and cottages, these now intermingle with the modern blocks of flats, houses and bungalows. Throughout the village are tree-lined avenues and roads. The shopping centre is set amid areas of grass with paved walkways; there are flowering trees, shrubs and flower planters. At Christmas time, the trees are adorned with hundreds of glittering lights, giving the village a fairytale atmosphere. The pebble and sandy beach is fine and safe for the children and for all seaside sports, including horse riding along the sands at low tide. Although Rustington is mainly residential, to the north of the village is situated what is known as the industrial estates, these range through a variety of light industrial units. Nationally known superstores are sited on the north-east of the village.

Despite all this, Rustington jealously guards its village identity, and in recent years, has twice fought off the prospect of being called a town, with a town council. Rustington has had many famous and notable people, who made the village their favourite holiday haunt or home.

Rustington has its own ghost stories, some of which seem to defy explanation. This, as well as tales of smuggling abound in the village. There are supposedly tunnels, which run from the older properties, like The Elms, The Manor House, Cudlow House, and Walnut Tree House, either to each other, to the church, the sea front or even to Angmering village. Smugglers yes, tunnels no, the water table is far too high, for any tunnelling to be done hereabouts. Certainly all the cellars of village properties here in Rustington, are fitted with their own pumps, in order to pump out the water when the cellars flood. Some odd underground storage places, which could have been hid-ing places for a few wine casks and contraband on a temporary basis, have been found in the village.

Rustington until a few years ago was networked with deep ditches, which were usually full of water for nine months of the year. I have been told that smugglers in special flat-bottomed boats paddled silently from one part of the village to another, along these convenient ditches. Certainly I have seen the remnants of a landing stage, alongside the banks of one of the ditches, which ran through the grounds of one of the larger houses in the village, which does seem to add credence to the story. The local smugglers were known as the Ragman Totts, this because of their habit of binding rags around the wheels of their carts and wagons, to help deaden the sounds of their approach.

Later, the local miller came in on the act, as if the revenue cutter or excise men were about, he would stop the sails of the mill, to form an upright cross, which could be seen for many miles around, and acted as a visual warning to 'The Gentlemen'.

1 Two prominent members of Rustington society in the past, a vicar and a solicitor, claimed that they had the original drawing hanging in their studies, however, this is as maybe. There have been many copies made of this sketch, which is interesting in that it is exact as to the positioning of the buildings, flint walls and gates, which were extant at the time. Much of the property details on the right side of the road have long since been demolished, to make way for the new Lamb Inn and car park.

" RUSTINGTON IN 1860 "

2 The two horses are standing by Jessamine Cottage stables. The date of the picture is about 1890. Jessamine Cottage was where the McDonald sisters, the village seamstresses, lived. It is still there, but very much altered. All the properties between this house and the church are gone, they were Rose Cottage, then the ancient long low building of the old Lamb Inn, and adjoining the tall inn keepers house and cobblers shop. A large house called The Elms behind the elm trees and flint wall on the left is still there.

3   This is the only remaining timber-framed and jettied building left in Rustington. It was earlier known as Old Farm, when it formed part of the estate of West Preston Manor, under Mr. Thomas Bushby. Mr. Henson was the farm bailiff, between the years 1860 and 1870. He lived here with his family, and they all told of how this house was haunted by the ghost of a lady, who always carried a jangling bunch of keys. The house is now called Pigeon House Farm. It took this name following its complete renovation in 1946 by Mr. Mariner.

4   Here we see the north side of the 11th-century Parish Church of St. Peter and St. Paul, which is situated in the centre of the village. In this picture we see both the north and west mediaeval porches, as well as the single-handed clock, which dates from 1769, although the clock only came and was fitted to Rustington church in 1905. The tower dates from 1170, its battlements added in 1661; this date can be seen, picked out in red brick, at the top of the west face of the tower. The little gate in the churchyard wall was closed up in the 1960s as being far too dangerous to use, with the ever-increasing traffic on this corner.

RUSTINGTON CHURCH. 1545.

5 A view of the lych-gate, taken from inside the churchyard, which is somewhat unusual, as most pictures were taken from various points outside. This lych-gate was constructed from the old roof timbers, taken from the church at the time of its restoration in 1860, by the then vicar, the Rev. Henry John Rush. The lych-gate replaced an old five-barred farm gate, which had served as the entrance to the churchyard for many generations.

Rustington Lych-Gate.

6 An interior shot of the church, showing three heraldic shields, on a beam high up above the chancel arch; two are much older than the third, and escaped destruction in the 1860 restoration. The left shield bears the arms of the Bishop of Chichester, the centre one bearing the arms of King Edward III. The right-hand shield has the arms of the Earl of Arundel. The origin of the shields is a mystery. On the left of the picture, one can see a curtained recess, for many years used as the vestries. New purpose-built vestries were erected on the south side of the church in 1958.

INTERIOR OF RUSTINGTON CHURCH

H.7246

7 This 1932 picture of the church choir was taken at Kedesh, Knightscroft Avenue, with choirmaster Mr. Tim Healey seated centre. He was appointed choirmaster at the end of 1930. At this time the choir was mostly ladies, but as they left for one reason or another, he replaced them with men and boys, gradually building up a wonderful choir. He married one of the ladies in the choir, Miss Dorothy Stickley, in 1935. Two years later, the first of the choir boys camps was held, when Mr. and Mrs. Healey took the boys for a weeks camping holiday in Highcliffe, Hampshire.

These camping holidays became an annual feature until 1974, apart from the war years. It was at the first camp held after the war, at Tillington Surrey, that the boys spontaneously made Mr. Healey an 'Uncle' by adoption. Since that time he was known by no other title by three decades of choirboys. Uncle Healey had to retire after the 1974 camp, due to ill health.

8 These multi-picture cards were very popular showing, as they do, five totally different views of the village; there are well over fifty different versions of these cards. I chose this one because it shows cows walking down Sea Lane to their home at Hobbs Farm; possibly milking time, in the bottom left-hand picture. The bottom right view is of the Parish Church. Top right a view of the beach, top left the Lido holiday camp showing the children's swimming pool. The centre picture shows the Old World cottages in The Street. The date of this postcard is 1938.

9   Known to all as the Old World part of the village, this is The Street looking west. On the left side we see a deep ditch and wide grass verge, with Walnut Tree House Barn and the house called the Balchins in the distance. On the right, a flint and thatched house called Little ffynches, which dates from 1717. It is very much altered from the earlier house, and the changes can be seen where the flint work alters on the side-wall. This also shows the original height of the cottage. It was in 1930, that the other storey was added. The house was originally called ffynches Farm; it then had a farm-yard on its western side, with fields and meadows on the north and east side.

RUSTINGTON, LOOKING WEST.

10   In this postcard we see Garden Cottage on the left, with Mitchell's Cottage on the right. This is possibly Rustington's most photographed and painted scene. In summer months one can usually see an artist seated on a little stool, on the grass verge opposite, with sketchpad and paint box. Mitchells Cottage is the earlier of the two, in fact in a map of the area in 1780, there is no Garden Cottage, only a flint-built wood store. So it was some years later, that it was enlarged to become a cottage in its own right. We have a photo of Garden Cottage, taken in 1920, when it was only half its present size. Both cottages today have beautifully decked flower gardens, even growing hollyhocks and other flowers in the grass verges, lining the road.

OLD COTTAGES, THE STREET, RUSTINGTON.   3425

11 Mum and Dad Lan-
gridge is how this old
couple verging on 80 years
of age were known, they
lived at Garden Cottage.
There is a lovely story, that
at the time of Queen Victoria's Jubilee, flags floated
everywhere in the village,
but poor Mum had no
flag, yet her loyal and re-
sourceful mind quickly
supplied a substitute. She
tied one of Dad's enor-
mous red and white spot-
ted handkerchiefs to her
clothes prop, with a huge
bunch of bluebells at the
top, and honour was satis-
fied.

12   This is The Grange in Sea Lane; it was built about 1815 for Mr. Geering Lane and his family. John Addis bought the property and land, on 5th April 1847 for £3,200. His daughter Mary was married on 29th August 1855 to Richard Denny Urlin, the Victorian lawyer, philosopher and writer; they came to make The Grange their home. Hilda, one of their daughters, was married on 29th November 1897 to Professor Flinders Petrie, the Egyptologist, at the parish church in Kensington. The couple went straight from the vestry door to Victoria Station, en route for Calais, Paris and Egypt.

The Grange was demolished in 1935, following the death of Miss Ethel Urlin. The Grange Way and Hobbs Way have sprung up on its grounds.

13   A step further along The Street, on the right is the little gate to Firs Cottage, and then the roof and chimneys of Old Orchard House / Croesswdy, previously known as the Firs Dairy Farm. On the left of the picture we see Pound Cottage and jutting out into the road, the flint-built walls of the village pound, for stray animals. We do not know when the first Pound was built, but it can be seen on the Goodwood Estate maps of 1780, long before the cottage which then took its name, was built. The Lord of the Manor, Mr. W. Gratwick, rebuilt the Pound in 1800. Near where the car is parked, is the entrance to Tithe Barn.

RUSTINGTON VILLAGE.   H.4042

14 Rarely seen by people passing along the road, is this lovely home, Old Orchard House / Croesswdy. This is the west front. As we have mentioned under a previous caption, this house was earlier a dairy farm, called The Firs. Some of the old dairy buildings have been incorporated into the existing house, the alterations can be seen in the different flint work, as well as the different roof levels. The house can boast of having had some interesting owners and occupiers, among these were the Garretts, of Suffragette fame, and Elizabeth Garrett Anderson, the first woman doctor. The present owner is a Freeman of the City of London.

15   From Tompkins Diary, 'June 10th. 1805. Mr. Olliver, bought the tythes of Rustington, for £8000. October 5th. 1807. At this time, sold my friend Mr. Olliver a piece of ground at Rustingon, called the Old Orchard, to build a barn on, to take up the tythes, for £35.' This barn had fallen into disrepair, by the beginning of the 20th century, so it was converted and added to in the early 1930s, to become the attractive residence it is today. It lies well back from the road, so it is rarely seen by anyone passing by. It is called Tithe Barn. It is probable that both Elm Cottage and Pound Cottage were built at the same period as the old Tithe Barn.

16   Carriage and pair coming down The Street, towards the Lamb Corner, about 1905. On the right we see the flint wall that surrounds the churchyard. The first building on the left is the carpenter's shop of Mr. C.J. Drake. Mr. Drake became one of the first property developers in the village; he was responsible for building the new Lamb Inn in 1902. He also built the majority of the houses in the village centre, Church Road etc. at the turn of the 20th century. The second building is where carriages kept for hire, were housed. The thatched barn was one of the few remaining buildings left from the farm that had once covered this area. It was called Quaker Smiths Farm, which was said to be very prosperous. All these buildings were swept away in the early 1930s.

17 Church Farm Cottages in The Street, a remnant of the old Quaker Smiths Farm. We see them with their south front covered in ivy. The left of the picture shows the open gate into the churchyard, sheltered by a huge horse chestnut tree, which stood here for well over a century. The village deliverymen on his three-wheeled bicycle appears to be handing the lady a newspaper. The finger post in the distance points out the road to Littlehampton. At the front right corner is the entrance to Church Road. The postcard dates from 1910.

Church Farm Cottages, Rustington.

18 Almost the same view as the previous picture, but some years later. The horse chestnut tree is still there, but now it shelters a telephone kiosk as well as the churchyard gate. On the right Church Farm Cottages, minus the ivy; at this time it had become the surgery and premise of Mrs. Dora Green, the veterinary surgeon. In the distance, all the farm buildings have long since gone, and in their place came a small parade of shops, known as Church Parade. This parade comprised of a hardware / cycle shop, a tobacconist / sweet shop, two well-known banks, an estate agent, a ladies' and gents' hairdresser's, and a butcher's shop.

RUSTINGTON - THE STREET (EAST)

19   Here in this picture we are looking up The Street in the 1940s. The churchyard wall is on the right and Church Farm Cottages are on the left. Next to this is a large house, with shop adjoining, which belonged to Mr. Stanford. It was a grocery provisions store, which roasted and ground its own coffee. Beyond the shop blind you can just pick out the sun umbrellas of the Victoria Farm Dairy. These were above tables and chairs, where you could sit and drink the most delicious milk shakes, or eat the home-made ice creams and fruit sundaes; how this brings back happy memories of my childhood! In the distance a 31 bus can be seen on its way to Worthing and Brighton. This part of The Street remained virtually the same, until the new shopping parades were built in the early 1960s.

RUSTINGTON VILLAGE.   H.7247

20 Rustington's Manor House, possibly the oldest house in the village; parts of it were found to be timber-framed, when undergoing restoration. Although it was owned by the Lord of the Manor since the start of the feudal system in the 11th century, it was mostly occupied by his tenant farmers. By the beginning of the 19th century, it had degenerated into a mere farmhouse. In 1869, it was bought by Mr. Heasman and became known as Heasmans Farm, it was then given over to occupation by his farm labourers and their families. Shortly after the First World War, the Count de Belleroche, a noted French artist and lithographer, bought the property, and restored it to something of its former grace. This picture about 1900 shows William 'Shep' Gates leaning over the wall with the village road sweeper.

The Old Manor House, Rustington.

21 This picture shows the south front of the Old Manor House, having undergone a major restoration in the 1950s. It then became The Manor Club, a licensed premises, which proved to be very popular for many social occasions, wedding receptions and other parties, having such a beautiful setting. When the Manor Club closed in 1991, it reverted to private ownership and became a splendid private residence. Part of its extensive grounds have been sold, however, with three houses built on that land, these having their own separate entrance, off Old Manor Road.

22   Mr. Simpson opened the first shop in the village in Sea Lane, as a bakery between 1833 and 1840, conveniently sited just around the corner from the Lamb Inn. Some years later, Mr. Simpson sold the shop to Mrs. Mary Ann Humphrey, who with the aid of her two sons ran the business for many years. I have been given to understand the shop sold everything you could want apart from drapery. She also opened the first post office here by 1881. This picture of 1908 shows one of Mrs. Humphrey's sons at the shop doorway, along with Mr. Bill Edmunds, one of the four Rustington postmen, who served the village. The shop is still there, and is now called House of Stitches.

23   We now see pictured the north end of Sea Lane, in the 1920s. On the left are the large white gates that gave entrance to the dairy and farmyard at Hobbs Farm. The farmhouse was built to replace an existing one on the same site in 1690. A date stone can still be seen, set high in the east wall of the house, with the initials R. and E. B. for Roger and Elizabeth Barwick, who were married that year, and came to live here. The farm takes its name from the Hobbs family, who were its owners in the 18th century. On the right, the cottages and small barn of Cudlow Farm can be seen. The cottages are still there, however, the barns and flint wall in the right foreground were swept away in the early 1930s, to form a new road called Cudlow Avenue, and when a small parade of shops was built here as well, they took the name of Cudlow Parade.

SEA LANE, RUSTINGTON.

24 The old barn is the only remaining farm building of the old Cud-low Farm. Many years ago, when it was still a hard-working farm, the barn was cleared out and twice a year hung with garlands and lanterns. It then became totally transformed to become the scene for lively parties, for many of the villagers who cared to attend. These parties were known as ' Kick the Can Night', and the Harvest Moon party. In the 1940s, following the Second World War, the southern most cottage and barn were bought by a dealer of antiques, he used the barn as a unique showroom.

THE OLD BARN CAFE, SEA LANE, RUSTINGTON.

25   Here in this postcard, we see an interior view of the old barn when converted to become the antique showroom, then incorporating a tearoom, this was about 1949. It became a very popular meeting place for coffee and teas; they also eventually ran to serving light lunches. However, in the August of 1952, the café side of the business closed, and the owner and his wife, concentrated on their antique business. Some years later, the barn was converted into a private two-storey residence and sold. It has recently again been on the market, at an asking price of £325,000.

INTERIOR OLD BARN CAFE, SEA LANE RUSTINGTON

26 A picture of how the southern end of Sea Lane looked in 1930. On the left, we see the entrance to Timbers Nursery, owned by Mr. Ben Rubenstein. He had a fine house built at the nursery. His wife was the famous operatic prima donna Conchita Supervia. They were married in 1930, but sadly their life together was short, she tragically died in childbirth in 1936, the baby boy dying with her. Behind the hedges further along is a house called Green Hedges, which was the home of Mr. and Mrs. Sutherland and their son Graham, who became a famous artist. A little further along and you come to Knights Croft House, the home for over forty years of the eminent musician and composer Sir Hubert Parry. He lived here with his wife Lady Maud Parry and their two daughters Dorothea and Gwendoline. The house is still there but now divided into flats. The entrance on the right leads to the Southern Star Service Station.

SEA LANE, RUSTINGTON.   9705

27　Here we see the Southern Star Service Station; it was opened and owned, by Mr. Hiscocks in 1928. The low building on its right was originally erected as a store for Professor Flinders Petrie, the famous Egyptologist, to house his artefacts. In 1921, it became a tearoom, for the adjoining tennis courts, owned by the Janes. In 1922 the Denyer's turned them into the Pavilion tearooms. Mr. and Mrs. Hiscocks purchased them in 1928, and they remained in their ownership for many years, until they sold them to Mr. and Mrs. Power, the tearooms then became known as the Smugglers Roost. It is now a very popular Free House and Licensed Restaurant. On the far right, can be seen tall buildings, this was the Millfield Convalescent Home, built in 1903, as a seaside home for children. It later became a convalescent home for children suffering from tuberculosis. It was demolished in 1958, and flats now stand on the site.

28 The Gates Sister's opened Rustington's first tearoom in 1901. Here we see, seated at the table, Mrs. Gates, being served tea and cakes by her niece Miss Daisy Gates. Mr. William Gates leans over the wall, while the pet goat is being fed by Mr. Gates' sister-in-law Lois. The two sisters started the tea room in premises built by their husbands, with only 2/6d (12½p) worth of mineral waters. Later they were able to serve tea and cakes, and the little business ran very successfully until 1913.

THE RUSTINGTON TEA ROOM.

29   Here we have a postcard view of Rustington House, Worthing Road. This was built about 1822 for Edward Greenfield Penfold, a barrister. He was responsible for the greater part of the land in Rustington being land registered. He was a very popular gentleman, and was known to all as the Squire. After his son Hugh Charles Penfold died in 1908 the property was sold to a Miss Hamilton. While she was in residence there, she held a large fête in the grounds, the proceeds of which she gave to the Women's Suffrage Movement. The subsequent owners of the House were Sir Malcome and Lady Fox, followed by Sir George Hutchinson, the publisher. During the Second World War it was commandeered by the military, as were so many Rustington properties. Following the war, Mr. Easter bought the house, but in 1949 it was sold again to the Electrical Trades Union, for use as a convalescent home for their members. In the late 1960s, it became the Rustington House/Summerlea School, and it remained a girl's school until it was sold in 1986. Today, the house is the H.Q. of the Hargreaves Construction Co.

30 As far as I am aware, this is the only known picture of one of Rustington's many brickfields, the date 1890. This one was owned by John Eade Butt. The site of this brickfield was in Worthing Road, and was at one time known as the Victoria Brick and Tile Works. In the middle distance you can see Victoria Cottage, later it was called The Anchorage. It was at this time the home of Mr. Shepherd, who was the manager, and most of his nine sons worked in the yard for their father. The house was demolished in 1962, to create space for the Artex Avenue industrial estate.

31 Here on the corner of Claigmar Road and The Street is the Rustington War Memorial, standing on a small portion of land, leased from the Methodist Church, which can be seen in the background of the photo. The Memorial, listing the names of the fallen in the two Great Wars, was unveiled by Admiral C. Caslon CB CBE RN on 6th July 1952 in the presence of all sections of the village community. Since that date, two further plaques have been added to the wings on both sides of the Memorial. One was set up to commemorate the Canadian soldiers who were stationed in the village during the Second World War. They were sent on a mission, with few returning; this was unveiled on 3rd September 1989. The right-hand side, which commemorates the 50th anniversary of the ending of the Second World War, was unveiled in 1995.

32   Here we are in the east end of The Street, full of trees, a quiet and peaceful residential area in the 1940-1960s. The house just peeping into the picture behind all the trees in the left-hand corner is still there minus the garden, but is now converted into a large electrical showroom. From where the two gentlemen are walking to the top of the picture it is scarcely recognizable today, it is all parades of shops both sides of the road. They have even made a zebra crossing, enabling you to cross the road in safety, with the constant streams of traffic now flowing in the village.

The Street looking East, Rustington.   1546.

33 The date of this picture is 1959. The house on the left was called The Croft. Dr. Waller lived and held his surgeries here. It was all so prim and Victorian, with stiff upright chairs, around the edge of the waiting room, copies of The Field, and Tatler, on the highly polished table. This house was one of three secluded houses swept away along with a large goat field, for developing the new shopping parades.

34   Here we see the Henson family, hard at work in the hayfield off of Broadmark Lane. We see one of the family's traction engines, helping with the task. The Hensons had by this time moved from Pigeon House Farm in Station Road to a farm called Trafalgar on the opposite side of the road, between Herne Farm and Allangate Cottage. Also in Station Road was the yard where the Henson's kept their threshing machines and other farming equipment.

35 A very nostalgic view of Ash Lane, also known as Broadmark Lane for a very short period. The finger post points the way to Littlehampton and Bognor, but few cars were seen in the village when this picture was taken, about 1921. The large house to be seen on the right was called The Matthews. In 1935 one of its front parlours was let out several hours each week to the Westminster Bank, while another room was let to Wellings Estate Agents. The Matthews was demolished in 1936, to be replaced by the Broadmark Parade of shops. Due to the onset of the Second World War, only a few of the shops and offices had been completed and let.

36 Ash Lane in the 1950s looking north, showing still only a handful of shops. These were Rita's small general drapers, haberdashery and toys, then Chesterman's general store and sweet shop, followed by Bookers the bakers, where then you could still get a bakers dozen, lastly a ladies' and gentleman's hairdressing salons, run by Mr. and Mrs. Bailey. Behind the row of trees was a small row of 1920s bungalows, they are still there today, only one of them has been converted to a doctor's practice. I am afraid the road is somewhat busier today than seen in this picture.

37   Here we are in Ash Lane again, looking south, in the 1920s. We see the hedges on the right of the goat field. On the left the handful of shops comprising the Stonefield Bakery, built by C.J. Drake and run by the Booker family. Next the house and shop which then was Wilmer's store, Rita's the drapers adjoins it on the right. In the distance you can see the Matthews with surrounding high flint wall, which jutted out into the pretty lane that led down to the sea.

BROADMARK LANE, RUSTINGTON.   1693

38 This postcard reads Broadmark Avenue, but this is incorrect, it is Broadmark Lane looking north. The picture shows the small thatched property called Bumble Cottage. Originally near here stood a little black wooden cottage with a cow shed. In 1878, the cowshed was pulled down and in its place was built the Bumble cottage we know today. Mrs. Simmonds and her son moved in, and their former home, the wooden cottage, was broken up.

BROADMARK AVENUE, RUSTINGTON.   D 13738

39 Broadmark Lane looking south. On the left is the entrance to Bushby Avenue, with the blacksmith's forge. The smithy had formerly been at the corner of The Street and Broadmark Lane, but had failed through bankruptcy. Two blacksmiths were known to have worked the Bushby Avenue forge, the first Jimmy Francis, followed by a Mr. Hubbard, who kept a pet parrot for company, the parrot must have found it remarkably noisy. This lane used to be known for its beauty, it had a deep ditch running down its west side, the banks of which were carpeted in spring, with violets and primroses. To reach what houses were built here, one had to cross over the ditch by means of small wooden bridges. The high hedges either side of the lane were a mass of wild rose blossom in summer, and colourful hips and haws in the autumn.

- BROADMARK LANE - RUSTINGTON. -

40 The postcard of Glenville Road in the 1950s shows the terrace of houses, built by Thomas Summers in 1899. While Tom built his houses, he allowed his wife to chose and name them all, a few of the houses still retain the names she gave them. The majority of those houses built by Tom Summers are known as being in the Broadmark Estates. The road leads from Broadmark Lane to the Zachary Merton Hospital. The road on the left is called Waverley Road, the road to the right leads to Amberley Road and Merton Avenue etc.

41   Here we see the Zachary Merton Maternity Hospital Rustington. The hospital was built in 1936 and opened on 23 April 1937. It was originally opened as a convalescent home for mothers, babies and toddlers, some time later it became a maternity hospital and held an enviable reputation for well over thirty years. Eventually the maternity hospital was scaled down, and finally closed in June 1979. The buildings reopened in November of that same year as a community hospital. The unusual name comes from the generous philanthropist, who gave a large sum of money, on the death of his wife, to be used for the founding of convalescent homes, Rustington was one of the sites chosen.

RY MERTON CONVALESCENT HOME, RUSTINGTON (SOUTH FRONT). 1544.

42 This 1926 postcard shows Woodbine Cottage in the snow. The cottage is situated at the junction of three roads, Mill Lane, Station Road an Ash Lane. On the east front of the house, there is a well- worn date stone showing the date of 1793. C.J. Drake added the right wing of the house in 1910 for the then owner, Mrs. Faulkner. The cottage was at one time a tearoom. Rustington certainly had its fair share of tearooms over the years. I was asked once, in all seriousness, if the cottage was named after Willie Woodbine, the answer is definitely no! It was originally named after the wild flower woodbine, an old name for honeysuckle.

43 A shady road is how this card is described, it certainly is a tree lined road, and as such is remarkably sad, as all these trees died, having caught the dreaded Dutch Elm disease. The road is in fact Station Road, earlier known as East Street, before the arrival of Angmering Station. The only thing that is recognizable and in the same position is the telephone kiosk. On the right is the entrance to the Parkway. The thick hedge on the left of the picture has gone, it is now the site of the Roman Catholic Church of St. Joseph, along with the Priest's House.

A Shady Road, Rustington

44 This picture of West Preston Manor when still in private ownership about 1930. We think the original house was a mediaeval hall house, with a central open chimney, which still exists. This has been adapted to serve two fireplaces, as well as retaining recesses for drying salt. The larger section of the house is partially Queen Anne and Early Georgian in construction, the different flint work of the two periods being readily distinguished. The south wing is about 1800, with fine flat knapp flint work on the south-facing wall. From the de L'Isle manuscripts we can trace the Manor's origins from Ralph de Ardern in 1230 and by other records until the present day. It was sold to a Miss Boykett in 1933, who then opened a school here later that year; it ran very successfully for 46 years, closing in 1979. Miss Boykett sold the Manor House and its grounds to the 'Help the Aged Association'.

45 The almshouse's were built about 1620, though not necessarily at the same time, for they were not alike, one being single-storeyed whilst the other had two floors. They were used as the Poor House of Rustingon, before the East Preston Union, or Workhouse, was built in 1872. It is interesting to discover that the Rustington boundary line ran behind these cottages, along the wall of the church, which itself was in East Preston, whilst the cottages were in Rustington. They were demolished in 1931, last occupied by Mrs. Cox and a Mrs. Mills.

46 A picture of Seafield Road in the early 1930s. These houses and cottages were built on land that was previously owned by Miss Urlin, who resided at The Grange. They were mainly used for holiday accommodation. There were also tennis courts here in 1927; open to non-residents, tickets cost 1/6d for 2 persons, 4 persons 2/6d, and the tickets were on sale at the Pavilion Tearooms. The worst destruction of the war to occur in Rustington was in Seafield Road, when on 8th May 1942, a bomb demolished a house on the south side of the road, and blast coupled with cannon fire damaged numberless houses to a greater or lesser degree. Two people were killed, five seriously injured, and many others had minor wounds.

Seafield Road, Rustington.

47 This building, almost on the beach, at the bottom of Broadmark Lane, was originally the Newton Driver Services Club, as seen in the picture. Prince Philip, the Duke of Edinburgh, opened the Club in April 1947. Many of the villagers turned out to welcome him to Rustington. Mrs. Newton Driver OBE founded the Services Club, in memory of her husband, for the use of disabled or convalescent servicemen. The Duke of Kent agreed to it being renamed Princess Marina House, after his mother, the Duchess of Kent. She had applauded its facilities and equipment when she had visited the club in 1962. It then became a home for ex-RAF personnel, when it was taken over by the RAF Benevolent Fund in 1969. The Duke of Kent opened the new wing in 1980.

NEWTON DRIVER SERVICE CLUB, RUSTINGTON.

48   Dozens of pictures were taken of the Lido and its amenities, this is one of the bathing pool. Mr. Sydney Jones had the Lido built in 1936. Reputed to have the first out-door roller skating rink, it also boasted a ballroom, conference hall, tennis courts and bowling greens, all set in 40 acres of grounds, that were floodlit at night, as well as having coloured fountains. Commandeered during the Second World War, by troops, mostly Canadian. In 1947, it was sold to the Workers Travel Association, and some ten years later it took the name Mallon Dene. The whole complex was demolished in 1968, and the Mallon Dene Estate put up on the site.

THE BATHING POOL, THE LIDO, RUSTINGTON.   H.724

49 The Broadmark Hotel was sited just south of the Lido, on the greensward, just above the beach. Unlike the Lido, it held a license to sell alcoholic drinks. This hotel too, was requisitioned by the military during the war, latterly by American troops. They gave the children of the local service men a wonderful Christmas party, the like of which few of us had experienced before. We all came home with loads of goodies, chocolate and fruit, as well as Christmas garlands. The Broadmark continued in use as a hotel and bar, until being demolished in 1984, and the Broadmark Flats were built on the site.

BROADMARK HOTEL, RUSTINGTON H.7265.

50 Rustington has a fine sandy beach at low tides, beach games as well as horse riding are very popular along these sands. The top of the beach is mostly shingle, with a tamarisk hedge running along the edge of the greensward. World air speed records were set up between Sea Lane Rustington and nearby Kingston Gorse, over the beach, on 7th September 1946. Group Captain Donaldson DSO.AFC. set up the first record flying a Gloster Meteor, then Neville Duke OBE.DSO and 2 bars, broke the record over the same timing points, on 7th September 1953, flying in a Hawker Hunter. On 7th September 1996, at a special ceremony held on the beach, Neville Duke watched a special flypast of a Gloster Meteor and a Hawker Hunter in front of an invited audience. He then unveiled a plaque on the greensward, to commemorate the 50th anniversary of these records. A reception was held at the village Memorial Hall.

The Beach, Rustington.

51 Sea Road, the Sea Mill and the Millfield Convalescent Home, in the year 1910. Incredible as it seems, this road from Rustington to Littlehampton was allowed to remain in this appalling condition until 1930, when a pavement was added at the same time as the road was made good. The road originally came into existence in 1830, in connection with the Littlehampton Chain Ferry, and its maintenance was the responsibility of the Ferry Trustees. This windmill was one of three that at one time worked in the village. This one lasted between 1821 and 1913.

52 All day on 4th March 1912 there was a great storm; the results of which were like all catastrophic occasions, very much photographed by the postcard firms, this one of Sea Mill being no exception. The hugely thick flint wall, which had been used as a sea defence – yes, even in those days – was no match for the lashing raging sea, in one of its more violent moods, everything in its way was swept away or smashed. Storms are no new thing along this part of the coast.

ROUGH SEAS
OFF RUSTINGTON MILL. 4-3-12.

53   A day later than the previous postcard, here we see the results of the storm, the windmill was never to work again and was taken down the following year. The sea wall lay scattered around the beach in hundreds of boulders. A second windmill and the oldest in Rustington, about 1615-1896, was a post mill. It had stood at the north of the village, at the junction of three roads, Mill Lane New Road and Worthing Road. A third mill stood only a short period in a field adjacent to Sea Mill. This had been an open trestle post mill, which stood here between 1848 and 1857; it was then transported, by means of a low trailer pulled by a team of horses to Fishbourne, where it ended its days.

AFTER THE STORM AT RUSTINGTON MILL MAR 5 1912

54   The Rustington Convalescent or Carpenters' Home is the largest building in the district, and possibly the finest, originally set in some 17,5 acres of land. It was built and endowed by Sir Henry Harben, who was Master of the Worshipful Company of Carpenters. The home was opened in 1897. Since that time dozens of postcards have been produced for the patients to send home to their families. This picture about 1910 shows the men wearing caps and boaters of that period. Centenary celebrations took place in the home in 1997, when a special commemorative booklet was produced.

45456. RUSTINGTON CONVALESCENT HOME.

55 The Convalescent Home's recreation room, as it looked in 1930. All the games are set out on the little tables, ready for the patients to enjoy, at their leisure. Note the old wireless set on the mantle piece. The home had every amenity, including a donkey cart, which transported the patients to and from the local station. The only time the home was closed was during the Second World War, when it was suggested that it should be used as a military hospital, but this was considered inadvisable, owing to the possible danger of the district being in the direct line of a German invasion. It was in fact requisitioned by the troops.

RECREATION ROOM, THE CONVALESCENT HOME, RUSTINGTON. H.7258.

56 The Rustington Silver Band was originally formed from a few members of the old Primitive Methodist Chapel Band. It grew to become a large band used regularly for local occasions. They played at the head of all the carnivals, which were held annually in aid of the local hospitals. They also played at Christmas time, for carols at various points in the village, as well as at other festivities and functions, like the Foresters Fair Day. This particular group had mustered for the Peace Day celebrations. In the picture we see from left to right as follows: Albert Denyer, George Yeates, Bert Vincent, George Voller, ?, Frank Hoare, George Field, Harry Gates, ? Young.

57 The four Rustington postmen pictured in 1905. These four posties in those days delivered and sorted all the mail themselves, working from Angmering Station, which then had its own postmark. The postmen are from left to right: Mr. Bill Edmunds, Mr. Corney, Jack Greysmark and Jack McDonald. In these days, the postmen carried a little pouch, in which to carry postage stamps, which they could sell to members of the public on outlying farms or houses. This practice was only discontinued in 1967. There is now a staff of 101, of whom 73 are actually on deliveries. Somewhere in the region of 25 million items of post are handled annually by the Royal Mail delivery office at Rustington. Mrs. Mary Ann Humphrey opened the first post office in Sea Lane by 1881.

58   Every town and village has its own football club, Rustington is no exception. The Rustington club was formed in 1903 and plays in the West Sussex League. This picture, taken for the year 1927-1928, shows the players with their manager, Mr. Atterbury top left. The team displayed the cup they had won to all; they have also brought along their doll mascot, I was told it was an oxo doll.

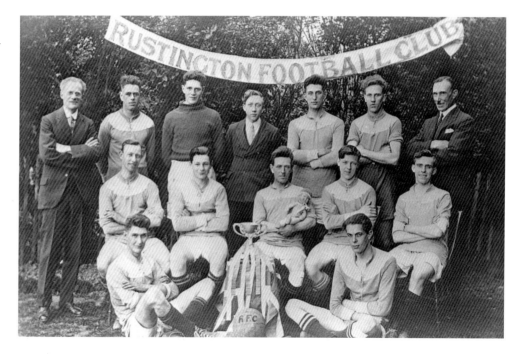

59 The Rustington Cricket team in 1920. At this time they played their matches on the Henry Avenue fields. The cricket team was founded in 1892, I only have the names of some of the players in the picture, and they are as follows, left to right: 1 White, 2 ?, 3 ?, 4 G. Wood, 5 Kepplewhite. Centre row: 1 Horace Booker, 2 Mr. Harding, 3 Frank Hoare, 4 Fred Mockford, 5 ?. Front row: Scorer, 1 Agnes Hoare, 2 Betts, 3 Eddie Woolven, 4 Fred Pelham.

60 Mewsbrooks House, an austere castellated building, was built by Robert Bushby in 1870 for Mr. Louis Barnes. The name Mewsbrooks derives from this area of land, which in documents from the Court Rolls of 1561 was called Mewes. When the Barnes family left the house in 1924, a Mrs. Bland bought it, and converted it into the Rustington Towers Hotel. Apart from every facility within the hotel, it also boasted stabling for six horses and garages for ten cars. The hotel grounds were vast and included tennis courts and croquet lawns. The hotel was gutted by fire in 1935; the only remaining part of the building was opened as a club, which ran for just a year.

'MEWSBROOK' LATER CALLED RUSTINGTON TOWERS.

61 Surprise as it maybe to some, this lake is built over the original delta of the River Arun, where the river entered the sea here many centuries ago. Until April 1933 it had remained a swampland. When Littlehampton took over this part of Rustington, they drained the area and built what is today the Mewsbrook Park boating lake. Other attractions here include a fenced-in children's play area, as well as a miniature railway line to Littlehampton, which is believed to have commenced operating in the summer of 1948.

MEWSBROOK PARK BOATING LAKE, RUSTINGTON D13756

62 The vicar Henry John Rush bought a piece of land freehold for £50. In 1859 he had a village school built on it. When it was completed, he conveyed as a gift, the school, schoolhouse and the land on which it stood, to the vicar, churchwardens and to the parish of Rustington. Here we see the school building on the right of the adjoining schoolhouse. It then saw a century of use as the village school; it still has a preparatory school operating here. The main purpose of the school buildings today, however, is as the church hall; they have been enlarged and modernized, to form the venue of many village activities and club functions.

This picture of the school building dates from 1899.

63 Group 2 children, who were attending the church school in 1918. An elderly gentleman gave me this picture of the school children, along with their names, he was one of these children. We have, left to right, back row: William Lee, Jack Seymour, Stella Stanbridge, Jim Betts, Sid Barnett, Eddie Woolven and Frank Stoner. Centre row: Ronnie Oliver, George Kilhams, Blanch Carter, Frank Morrallee, Helen Short, Eddie Lee and Dorothy Carter. Front row: Frank Kingshot, Rosy Weller, Ronnie Lee, Winnie Rowe, George Stanbridge and Jack Kingshot.

64 These happy children had their photo taken in the field of the North Lane School in the 1960s. Mr. Williams is the teacher, top left, next to my second son Graeme. This school, which opened in 1939, was the first of the three primary schools to open in the village, the second was Georgian Gardens, situated in the east of Rustington, to cover this part of the village. The latest, the Summerlea School, for the north catchment area, took its name from the girls' school, that had been at the nearby private school in Rustington House.

65   During the Second World War, Rustington like every town and village had its LDV Dad's Army, as it is now popularly called. Here we see a hand full of them, driving along Station Road, on Jimmy Piggott's pony and cart. Jock Wadley, the local tailor, is seen on his bike, Bill Williams is on the back of the cart, the pony's name was Bimbo. Jimmy with his pony and cart, was a familiar sight in the village in the early years of the war as the Home Guards unofficial transport. The house in the background was originally built in 1918, as the Depot Office, at the entrance to the American Air Base.

Some years later it served as the Shirlands Guest house, later hotel and club. In 1961, it was sold, and redeveloped into flats.

66 Rustington Home Guard in 1940 comprised one platoon, no. 7 'C' coy, 6th Battalion, having four sections, each with 30 men, together with H.Q. personnel. Two officers were appointed and granted regular army commissions, when the local strength was up to 130 volunteers. By June 1942, the strength in the home guard was 170 men, with four officers. This picture is of no. 3 section, Sergeant C. Cox is seated centre front wearing a forage cap and holding the cup. They had won it for an 'Assault at Arms,' inter section competition, held on 2nd August 1941.

67   By the summer of 1940, there was a possibility of a German invasion called Operation Sea Lion along this part of the coast. The village was at threat, so most of the children were hurriedly moved away. The beach was closed, and the use of the Sea Road to Littlehampton, was denied the public. Buses were diverted along North Lane and Worthing Road for the duration. The seafront became a fearsome looking place, having huge concrete blocks, miles of rings of barbed wire fencing, scaffold poles built into barricades, interspersed with concrete pill-boxes. The foreshore was sewn with landmines, and a particularly imposing blockhouse sprang up at the end of Sea Lane, this can be seen in this picture. Other barricades were constructed at all junctions into the village, which became a restricted zone.

68   This about 1946 picture of the ladies of the Rustington branch of the W.V.S. shows the ladies who did so much for the war effort. Their names we have from information received are as follows. Back row, left to right: 1 Mrs. Newman, 2 Mrs. Cooper, 3 Mrs. Warby, 4 ?, 5 Mary Churcher, 6 ?, 7 Mrs. Walker, 8 Zoe Campbell, 9 Mrs. Ireland and 10 Mrs. Standen Thomas.

Front row: 1 Miss Stevens, 2 Kathleen Hiscocks, 3 Mrs. Strass, 4 Joan Patterson, 5 lady in white chair is Mrs. Kathleen Ingersol, 6 Mrs. Magnus Osborne, 7 ?, 8 Bridget Reid and 9 Mrs. Stromwell. The lady in the front is not known.

69 The Fletcher Arms is situated in Station Road, almost opposite Angmering Station. This public house was converted from Munmere Cottage, which had been the home of Mr. Warren, a fly proprietor, who kept carriages to take passengers to and from the station. It then became the Fletcher Arms in 1936. The Thomas family were the first licensees of this public house, and it remained in the hands of the same family until 1977. Incidentally, Station Road only became known as this when the railway line came in 1846, prior to this time it had been known as East Street.

70   Here we have a picture taken at the foot of Windmill Bridge, which shows the home-made bakery, and the Old Windmill Inn. Both take their name from the post mill, which stood close by. The cottage was reputed to have been built in 1613; it is certainly consistent with the period, being constructed with timber framing, and having wattle and daub walling, as well as an inglenook fireplace. It became an inn about 1829. The buildings are still there today, having been converted into two cottages; they are no longer thatched, however. In its day, the pub had a skittle alley, along with tea gardens, which had small thatched arbours scattered about the pretty garden.

71 This is the new Windmill Inn, constructed as a purpose-built inn, for Messrs. Henty and Constable in 1909. This inn was built next to the old Windmill Inn and opposite where the windmill used to stand. This picture proudly displays its name above the window, although I have not seen this in any other picture. Mr. Herbert Ralph Booker was the first licensee of this public house. The Taylor Cup, awarded for the best floral display in the business class in Rustington, was won for the year 2000 by this public house.

72 The Lamb Inn was rebuilt in the year 1902; previously it had only been a long low single-storeyed building. In this about 1920's picture we see in the centre the large hall, which had a variety of uses over the years. These ranged from occasional use as the mortuary, for smoking concerts to which no ladies were allowed to attend, wedding receptions, committee meetings and latterly as a three-tabled billiard hall. It was pulled down in 1959 for road widening purposes, which never took place. The first post office in the village can also be seen on the left of the picture.

73 A carnival picture from 1920 is a must, Rustington was always noted for its annual carnivals, when all the money raised at the event, was given to the local hospitals. These always formed up outside the Lamb Inn. The colourful and lengthy procession formed of horse-drawn floats, decorated wheelbarrows, bicycles, with adults and children in fancy dress, would traverse the village of Rustington as well as East Preston, with the Rustington silver band leading the way. Here we see young boys just standing about, taking in all that is going on. It is said that as soon as one carnival was over for the year, every one went home, with an idea of what they were going to dress as in the next, such was the level of their involvement with the life of their village in those days.

74   Rustington Village Hall was built in 1938. Mr. C.D. Pinchin opened the hall on 12th October 1938, dedicating the hall to the memory of those who fell during the First World War, as well as commemorating the Silver Jubilee of King George V and Queen Mary. In 1986, as the hall being typical of the 1930s era, it was used for scenes for the David Leyland film 'Wish You Were Here,' starring Emily Lloyd and Tom Bell. Since that time the hall has been modernized, along with the kitchen, cloakroom facilities etc. To the rear of the hall, a new additional suite comprising of a small hall, committee rooms, kitchen, cloakrooms, storerooms, along with the Parish Council complex, have been added. The Rustington Heritage Association have an exhibition centre and office adjoining.

75 The Street from Chapel Corner – the picture taken in the year 1950 – may puzzle many people, who are relatively new to Rustington, and find it rather difficult to place.

This Primitive Methodist Chapel stood four feet out into the main road, and in its latter years had presented something of a traffic hazard. Originally it had been the village blacksmith's forge. It was converted in 1878, to become the Methodist chapel and had remained as such until 1952. It was removed in November of that year, when a new Methodist church was built in Claigmar Road. If you look at the following picture, plate no 76, its position should become clear.

76 This illustration comes from a similar viewpoint to the previous postcard of The Street, no. 75. This one was taken only ten years later. I am sure you will find it difficult to realize, that this is in fact the same stretch of road, so immense is the change that has taken place, with new parades of shops lining the road, replacing the trees, fields and the few houses that then comprised The Street. The Chapel would have been approximately where the nearest lamp standard stands on the left-hand side of the road, almost at the corner of the road junction.